From Teen To Palace

Walking In Your Destiny

Marina Abraham

xulon PRESS

11-11-17

GENERAL OVERVIEW

The book speaks to teenagers and describes how they can nurture the seed of greatness that God has given them and fulfil their potential by following His Word. Using scripture and personal experience as examples, the author motivates the reader to plan ahead, set goals, make positive choices, develop character, obey God, and seek out wisdom to ensure they are headed in the right direction.

DEDICATION

To God my creator, thank you for your unfailing love for me, for choosing me as a vessel worthy of your use. I return the glory for this work to you my Father.

To my jewel of inestimable value, a personal source of encouragement and inspiration, my darling husband, Samuel Abraham, remain in your palace and bless your generation.

And to all the "young people" throughout the world for whom I write this book, that you may come to know Jesus Christ, the only one who can truly help you to learn and abide by the principles that will enable you to reach your palace.

ACKNOWLEDGEMENTS

A s I say in this book, the company you keep has an influence on how you think and who you become. *From Teen to Palace* is a result of the people I have built my life around, the books I have read, and the men and women of God in my life. I am grateful for the prayer, nurturing, inspiration, encouragement and support of my company.

Family is everything, so I say:

- a big thanks to my mother for denying herself and giving me the best to make me the woman I have become.
- to Samuel my husband, I am eternally grateful to you, for being the earthly angel that keeps watch over me and supports my dreams and aspirations, I love you always.
- I am grateful to my siblings, Angela Omoruyi, Elizabeth Opeche, Eugene Omoruyi and Kay Edokpayi, for all their love, support, encouragement and prayers. I love you and couldn't have wished for more from God.
- my amazing brothers-in-law: Sam Opeche and Osayamen Edokpayi: thank you for your love. You are the best!

- my sister-in-law, Sherryann Sue Omoruyi, you are a star and an encourager. I love you.

I could not be where I am without my spiritual parents and family:

- I am grateful for the mentorship of my General Overseer in the Redeemed Christian Church of God, Pastor E.A. Adeboye. Sir, you are a real gem. May God bless you for your teachings and true following of Jesus our Lord and Saviour.
- The late Dr Myles Munroe, Pastor Sunday Adelaja and many other great men of God whose books and teachings have inspired me: thank you for being a blessing.
- My pastor, Pastor Akin Komolafe. Thank you for your fatherly love and support. Your prayers over all the years are being answered, sir.
- Evangelist Osaretin Enabulele: thank you for your love, prayers and support. You always call my family at the very moment when we need an encourager. This book is one of the products of your encouragement. God bless you richly, sir.
- All members of the Africa Christian Fellowship, you are a true family. Thanks for your prayers and support all these years.
- All members of RCCG Jesus Disciples Centre, Newbury. You have been an awesome family to be with. Thank you for your prayers and support.

To my supporters in this vision:

- My dear friend June Bugenyi, I appreciate your sisterhood and support, both financially and with words of encouragement to see this vision and dream come true. I wish you all good gifts from above.
- My editor and now a friend, Juliet Belderbos, you are gifted and excellent in your job. Thank you for working so hard to bring this book to life. I was stuck until I met you. You are amazing!
- Lauretta Pilch, my friend and sister from another mother; you have been of great help, and support to me and believe in me so much. Thank you for your encouragement and support through the years, especially for the vision of this book.
- I am so indebted to all my friends and family in the UK whom I have not mentioned by name. You guys rock! Thank you for your friendship and love. I would not experience a palace life without your support.

PROFILE

———⬥———

Marina Abraham is, married to Pastor Samuel Abraham, and is an author, lawyer, youth pastor and leader. She is co-founder of Personal Potential Discovery. She is a motivational speaker, educator, writer, coach and mentor. She was awarded a Law degree from the University of Benin (Nigeria) and a Masters in Legal Practice from BPP University (UK), as well as diplomas in Ministry and Youth Ministry, from Christ the Redeemer College and Christian Youth Ministry respectively. She is passionate about young people and works tirelessly in supporting them to achieving their dreams. She is a role model to many young people in Nigeria and across the UK.

You can follow Marina Abraham on her blog @ oduware-abraham.blogspot.co.uk

FOREWORD

If all we have is what we see here and now and there is no promise for the future, then what hope is there? It is the vision of a desirable future that infuses a person with enough enthusiasm to pursue their dreams on a daily basis.

Marina engages the imagination of young people in a way that is tailored towards equipping them with the life skills that most young people of today need so dearly, if they are to reach the place of prominence set aside for them by God. She draws from her wealth of experience in working with young people over the years to present 'old truths' in a way that is not just contemporary but also attuned to the language of young people.

Sometimes it seems as though the destiny of many young people is stifled or on hold, and many more languish in a state of despair due to a lack of proper guidance and counsel. But that is about to change!

In this book, Marina confronts these social maladies head-on, and offers tried-and-tested methods to help young people paint a picture of a world that is within their grasp. A world where their potential is maximised. A world where their lives have relevance. A world where they do not have to settle for second best. A world from Teen to Palace.

The discoveries they will make about themselves will help them spread their wings for a flight to glory. Just see what you can do!

Sam Opeche is an award-winning gospel artist and the author of *Find Your Significance through The G.A.T.E.S of Life* and *Today is Good–Stories from my Stepmother*. He is the co-founder of The Marriage Workshop, a ministry that is dedicated to seeing marriages thrive despite the current societal challenges, and specific difficulties in individual marriages.

CONTENTS

Forward xv

Introduction xxiii

CHAPTER 1   THE SEED OF GREATNESS 27
The origin of man

What is the seed of greatness?

You too have the seed of greatness

What happens when we leave our seed idle?

Your seed of greatness is for the benefit of others

Identify your seed

Steps to identifying your seed of greatness

You can create

CHAPTER 2   IT STARTS FROM THE MIND 40
Your mind is a gift

Creation begins in the mind

Positive against negative thoughts

Your thoughts form your habits

Faith and thinking

Your dreams and your mind

Practical steps to develop your thinking

CHAPTER 3   PLAN FOR INTENTIONAL GROWTH 49
How we grow

Intentional growth needs determination!

Start today

Intentional growth is not drastic

Intentional growth helps you stay on track

Some parents are intentional about their children's growth

9 steps for intentional growth

CHAPTER 4   SET GOALS IN YOUR LIFE 58

What is goal setting?

Why set goal?

6 steps to setting and achieving the right goals

Smart

CHAPTER 5   MAKE THE RIGHT CHOICES 66

What are choices?

Your choices can make or break you

The consequences of your choices

Let nothing stop you from making good choices

Choose to take responsibility

Your choices are tied to your destiny

How to make good choices

Some practical steps to consider in your choice-making

CHAPTER 6   SEEK KNOWLEDGE 75

What is knowledge?

Where to acquire knowledge

Beware of false knowledge

CHAPTER 7   GROWING IN WISDOM 82

What is wisdom?

Sources of wisdom

9 ways in which God's wisdom is worth more than gold

How to obtain divine wisdom

CHAPTER 8   MOVING WITH THE RIGHT PEOPLE 89

Your environment affects you

Choose your environment carefully

Find like-minded people

The risks of moving with the wrong crowd

CHAPTER 9   DEVELOP THE RIGHT CHARACTER
                         AND ATTITUDE. 95

The benefits of being of good character

How a bad character can hold you back

Characteristics to strive for

Role models

How your attitude influences your character

Character can be developed

CHAPTER 10   OBEY GOD. 103

Know God

What God wants

Prayer is the key

Prevalent sins amongst teens

Sex is a precious gift

Consequences of pre-marital sex

Abuse of drugs and alcohol

Help to stay pure

Reject all sin

The choice is yours today

PREFACE

Parents and grandparents are always looking for books that will help the teenagers in their lives follow God's Word and find success. The teen years are filled with difficult decisions and crossroads, so this age group often needs extra support. This book will appeal to teenagers who want a closer relationship with God and ensure that they live up to His expectations.

The author writes with a friendly and conversational tone that feels welcoming and approachable. There is still an air of authority and confidence present, which is important when offering advice. By using powerful, strong language, readers will feel empowered to take control of their lives.

The included advice is inspiring and broad enough to apply to many different situations and personalities. Important terms are defined, scripture is explained, and personal experience is given, which all support the main purpose of the book. The author presents a well-rounded source of motivation for any teen looking for the right path toward God and happiness.

INTRODUCTION

Y ou are born a royal

The story that brought about this book dates back to 2012. In wanting to walk more closely with God, my husband and I attended a one-year Christian Leadership course which transformed us. It transformed the way we think and the way we see ourselves. It brought us to a place where all we want to do is fulfil God's mandate for our lives. We learned that we are not here on earth by accident; we are here for a purpose (God's plan for our lives) and that every human being needs to understand their purpose and fulfil it while on earth.

I have always had a passion for helping young people. Little did I know that it was my calling and purpose until I attended that training. Now I am the youth leader at my church, and for the last two years, I have helped run a youth café in my neighbourhood. I visit some young people in their homes for one-to-one life coaching.

It breaks my heart when I see the young looking for meaning in their life but not finding an answer. I feel sad when they get caught up in things that won't lead to a bright future: violence, truancy, substance abuse to name but a few. These menaces hold so many of our youth back from becoming who they were created to be.

I see amazing teens with great potential, but something is missing in their approach to life and where they are heading. For example, some of the young people I know are still hanging out at 11pm in the street, even when they have exams the next day. I just pray for God to guide and help them. They often don't seem to see that there is more to life than just today, so they don't prepare for a more rewarding future.

THE JOURNEY OF FROM TEEN TO PALACE

I began to think about the conversations I'd had with some of them, about the things they say that they do at school: how they are rude to their teachers, disruptive in class, expelled even. What worried me even more was that I knew these are problems facing youths all over the world. They engage in such behaviours in a bid to find their identity, and some of them get lost on the way. Trying to heal this pain, I realised that God was laying on my heart to write a book that could reach those places I can't reach in person. A book that could show youths the principles that will help them to become who God has created them to be, expose them to the truth that they may otherwise not hear until they are adults, by which time the world seems to have shut down on them. The earlier a teen learns the right principles for life, the greater they become.

Some days later I was wondering what to call the book and I got the revelation clearly, 'From teen to palace'. In 1 Peter 2:9, it states that we are royals. We belong to the greatest kingdom that exists. We belong to the Kingdom of God, and as such, we have been born to rule and reign on this earth. This earth can be our palace but only those who live God's truth will have this 'palace experience' in their lifetime. There are steps to be taken to succeed in life.

This book is intended to provide you (teenagers and young adults) with some basic steps you can take to make your lives worthwhile and meaningful, rather than merely an existence.

I believe most people want to be the best they can be in life. We all dream of success, whether in sport, politics, music, family life, study, charity work.... the list of possibilities is endless.

As Christians, we are expected to be prayerful by default, and expect answers to our prayers. But our God is a principled God and to enjoy His blessing we need to follow His principles too. The people you admire didn't achieve their success by luck or magic. It was the result of following principles.

WHAT PRINCIPLES?

Principles are the values by which people live their lives. Choosing whether or not to follow certain principles can have profound consequences in the future.

When we refer to principles in this book, we refer firstly to Biblical principles as given by God, and secondly, those principles learned in our families, schools, churches, communities and society that help us grow from one stage to the next.

As a royal teen, your dwelling place should be the palace. Engage in what it takes to get there. As you read through this book, take action. You cannot say, 'Oh yeah, I know I will be successful,' and then fold your arms and wait for success to come.

By reading this book, you will clear away the clutter that can lead to life-altering mistakes. It will shine a light down the righteous path for you, covering how to:

- identify your seed of greatness
- change the way you think
- create goals that work for you
- seek out the wisdom you need to succeed
- follow God's plan for your life
- develop your character
- choose who to surround yourself with in your journey

CHAPTER 1

THE SEED OF GREATNESS

———⟨⟨❖⟩⟩———

'And God said, "Let us make man in our image, after our likeness.' -Genesis 1:26

Y ou may have read this scripture before; it is in the first chapter of the Bible. Maybe you have heard it preached in church or shared in your home? If you were like me as a teenager, you would have had to memorise it as a scripture for the day.

What does this scripture mean to you? How much have you allowed it to affect the way you live your life on a daily basis, whether at school or at home? In this chapter, we are

The Bible is a life manual for people who believe in Jesus. It's the Word of God to help us walk through life.

going to shed more light onto its meaning and help you see how it applies to you personally.

Perhaps it is the first time you have come across this text. Or maybe you don't know anything about the Bible at all? The Bible is a life manual for people who believe in Jesus. It's the Word of God to help us walk through life.

A lot of people, not just teens, struggle to understand the meaning of this Scripture in a practical sense, even if they have heard or read it numerous times. I used to be like that too. It was not until 2012 that I really understood its meaning, and it changed my life around.

I will try to illustrate it with a story I heard of a young man. One month into his first year of university, the class needed to choose a class representative (prefect) and they appointed him. But he said to them, 'Sorry, I can't do it; I don't have what it takes to lead'. He pointed to two other people whom he believed could lead better, but they insisted that the first man took the position.

One said, 'We chose you because we have been watching you in class, and think that you don't realise what great potential you have! You hardly contribute to a conversation; you lack confidence in yourself–but we believe that you can lead us.' So he reluctantly took the position and by the end of their third year, he had done tremendously well with the group and with himself. In those three years, he learnt to do things he didn't know he could do, even becoming president of the student union.

A lot of young people today are like this young man. They do not know who they are and what they are made of. They do not realise how much potential they have.

THE ORIGIN OF MAN

The story of the origin of man is found in the Bible, in the Book of Genesis 1:26. Unlike every other thing God created (for example the animals, who are said to have come from the land in Genesis 1:24), when God decided to create man, He didn't look at other things He had created, instead He looked at Himself.

When God decided to create man, He didn't look at other things He had created, instead He looked at Himself.

He knew He wanted to replicate Himself on earth, so that as He took charge in heaven, man would take dominion on earth, being His representatives and doing things as He would have done. God breathed His life into the nostrils of man, that humans may have the Spirit and life of God. Therefore, man is created in the 'image' of God. He has been given the special assignment of taking dominion over everything else that God created.

From this scripture, we can see that every man has the DNA of God, created to be just like Him. No matter how small a person may be, whether in age or size, that person has been created to be like God.

Man has the DNA of God, created to be just like Him. No matter how small a person may be, whether in age or size, that person has been created to be like God.

There are however a few characteristics of God we cannot possess. For example, God is present everywhere, which is why He is called omnipresent, but man can only be present in one place at a time. God never changes; He is the same yesterday, today and forever, but man is born and grows in stature, wisdom, and age. God does not die, He lives forever; yet the body of a man dies, though his spirit lives on.

And of course, God is without sin. He is pure love. Yet we sin. We let people down, we lie. God never lies; what He says He will do, He surely does.

> *God put a seed of greatness into everyone He created.*

God put a seed of greatness into everyone He created.

WHAT IS THE SEED OF GREATNESS?

A seed of greatness is your God-given gifts and abilities. It is who you are, your uniqueness, what distinguishes you from others. It is a treasure that makes you function in excellence like God does in heaven. Words like 'potential', 'gift', 'the real you', 'your treasure' are used to describe your seed of greatness. It is inside you. A lot of people drift through life because they do not know who they are and what they carry.

Every child of God – man, woman and child – on earth has something unique in them.

This seed becomes great when it is put to use, bringing fulfilment and satisfaction to you in life, providing goods and services for the benefit of others, and giving you both earthly and heavenly rewards. Its greatness is like looking at a forest and wondering how it came about, only to be amazed to know that it was one seed that sprang forth into many others and germinated to make a forest. Everything that is needed to make the forest was in one seed. Just as everything necessary for an acorn to grow into an oak tree is in the seed, so do you have this invisible seed deposited in you from conception to help you out live the purpose for which you were created. God's plan is for these seeds to grow, mature and blossom, so as to help you carry out your assignment on earth.

> *God's plan is for these seeds to grow, mature and blossom, so as to help you carry out your assignment on earth.*

Everyone's gifts are unique, setting them apart in their life or career. For example, Tiger Woods' seed of greatness is his ability to play golf. Serena Williams' seed of greatness is her ability to play tennis. Billy Graham's seed of greatness is his ability to preach the gospel in a simple yet very powerful way to bring people to God. Scientists (and all those who invent things for the good of their fellow men) all tap into their seed of greatness to make the world a better place.

YOU TOO HAVE THE SEED OF GREATNESS

A lot of people, especially the young, do not know that they have this potential, thus it is wasted, and they become frustrated when they are older. Our God is a God of potential, and because we are in His image and likeness, we have potential in us. That potential is what comprises of the seed of greatness.

> *Our God is a God of potential, and because we are in His image and likeness, we have potential in us.*

I hear you say, 'But Marina, how come that boy is a low-life, jailed for theft? Or that homeless man on the street? If they have the seed of greatness, how did they end up like that?' Everyone has the seed of greatness, but to attain greatness, every person needs to know and activate this seed. The starting point is discovering what your seed of greatness is, and it is this that will bring you to the palace.

WHAT HAPPENS WHEN WE LEAVE OUR SEED IDLE?

A quote which blew my mind (and helped me discover my seed of greatness) is by the late Dr. Myles Munroe, a great man of God and writer who influenced his generation in a tremendous way. He said, 'The wealthiest place in the world is not the gold mines of South America or the oil fields of Iraq or Iran. It is not the diamond mines of South Africa or the banks of the world. The wealthiest place on the planet is just down the road. It is the cemetery. There lie buried companies that were never started, inventions that were never made, bestselling books that were never written, and masterpieces that were never painted. In the cemetery is buried the greatest treasure of untapped potential.'

The outcome of many people's lives is so contrary to the purpose of God. A lot of people go to their graves with all the potentials that God gave them to place them in the best positions in life and also be a blessing to their generation.

YOUR SEED OF GREATNESS IS FOR THE BENEFIT OF OTHERS

As a teen, you are at just the right stage to prepare the ground of your life to become the great man or woman God has created you to be.

Ephesians 2:10 states that—we are God's workmanship, created to do good works. God made you specially and deliberately, with the potential to benefit others on this earth. As a teen, you are at just the right stage to prepare the ground of your life to become the great man or woman God has created you to be.

Proverbs 18:16 says that 'a person's gift opens doors for him, bringing him access to important people.' In the book of Genesis, chapter 40, we read about the young man Joseph who was in prison when he began to use his gift of interpreting dreams. One day, he was invited to interpret dreams for Pharaoh, the king. He moved from prison to palace, and from teen to palace! You can too!

All you need to do is have this understanding, early enough in your life, that no two persons are the same and that there is a seed of greatness inside of you that distinguishes you from any other person in your family, your peers or your best friends.

When you identify and nurture your seed of greatness, people will recognise it in you and come to you for solutions to their problems. I want to believe that you are excited about being that young man or woman whom people come to when they have specific needs. Joseph must have been excited when he interpreted dreams for his fellow prisoners, and it was one of them who brought Joseph to the king's attention when the need arose.

When you identify and nurture your seed of greatness, people will recognise it in you and come to you for solutions to their problems.

No matter how late as a teen you may think you are starting, it is never too late. Some begin this journey even at seventy. But the good thing is that you do not have

> *Developing your seed brings out your gifts, and your gift brings you to your palace*

to wait until seventy. The earlier you start, the better.

Nick Vujicic, 'the man without limbs,' is someone who inspires me. As a teen, he discovered that even though he had no limbs, he still had a seed of greatness inside him. He developed it and today Nick preaches the gospel and has met with presidents of the world! He is a motivational speaker and is transforming lives. He runs a charity through which he is giving back to the world, blessing his generation. This man had the choice of living in self-pity, but he chose to look within and find his unique seed of greatness.

Developing your seed brings out your gifts, and your gift brings you to your palace.

IDENTIFY YOUR SEED

Suzy is a close friend of mine. She worked in banking for many years, but never felt inner satisfaction. On her way home from work she would see young girls hanging about in the street, and her heart bled for them. She decided to set up a club where they could come together and be supported. Many girls who had been written off by their parents and community were transformed. Suzy found such fulfilment in her new work that she resigned from her job, took a course in youth coaching and today she continues to see many young people turn over a new leaf.

When you have not discovered your unique potential, your future is limited. You will just go with the flow and end up getting frustrated in life. Like Suzy, you may be busy doing something that pays the bills, but you will not be happy.

I have seen young people drift away. Do not be like that. You can do something with yourself! You are born to be a servant-leader. To serve your world in the area of your own gifts.

STEPS TO IDENTIFYING YOUR SEED OF GREATNESS

There are many ways to discover your seed of greatness, but I will introduce you to the three most important:

1   HAVING A RELATIONSHIP WITH YOUR CREATOR

Learn about God and communicate with Him. Follow His leading. In Jeremiah 1:5, God said, 'Before you were formed in your mother's womb, I knew you…' God knows you, and he knows what He has put inside of you!

You may say, 'But I go to church. Is that not enough?' No! To have a relationship with God is not about coming from a Christian home and church attendance alone. It is taking the personal decision to accept Jesus into your life (John 3:3), talking to God through prayer, learning to hear from Him, dwelling in the Word of God through reading the Bible. It is a personal choice that needs to be taken by an individual.

As Pope John Paul II said, 'It is Jesus who stirs in you the desire to do something great with your lives, the will to follow an ideal, the refusal to allow yourselves to be ground down by mediocrity, the courage to commit yourselves humbly and patiently to improving yourselves and society.'

2   WHAT CAUSES YOU PAIN?

What are the things that cause you pain or make you angry? The famous missionary Mother Teresa was filled with such sadness when she saw the poor and homeless, she left her teaching profession to start feeding and caring for them.

What is it that you would like to change, if only you could? This might be a clue to your seed of greatness.

3   WHAT DO YOU ENJOY DOING?

Pay attention to those things that give you joy when you do them. The things that give you satisfaction, even when no one pays you for doing it.

I know that I have numerous gifts, but the one that stands out is the desire to see young people become who they were created to be. This helped me to know that I am created to be a helper/encourager/agent of transformation to the young generation, and I do this for free for many young people.

YOU CAN CREATE

As a person made in the image of God, you have the power to create. What fruit will your seed bear?

I hear you saying, 'But Marina, I want to work in banking; what can I create with that?' That is an excellent aspiration, but the best you can become in life is not just to work in banking.

> *As a person made in the image of God, you have the power to create.*

You can use those skills and experience to establish your own company, or to create new systems, or transform the banking industry. Perhaps your generous salary can be saved to provide scholarships for disadvantaged children to go on to higher education?
Yes, you can work in banking, but your seed of greatness can also do more!

Whatever career you choose, you can be the best and leave a footprint. A lot of people drift into careers without thinking, or follow their friends, or do what their parents expect of them. And many people make mistakes, or keep changing course throughout their lives.

Imagine how fruitful it would be if every teen found the life they were created to pursue. The world would be a beautiful place.

The first principle for moving from teen to palace is to understand that you have a seed of greatness inside of you. You must identify it, nurture it and put it to use.

APPLICATION

As teens you need to take active steps today to make this happen. No-one can do this for you! Why not take some time to think through and begin to identify your seed of greatness.

CHAPTER 2

IT STARTS FROM THE MIND

———⌒⟡⌒———

'... but be transformed by the renewing of your
mind...'–Romans 12:2

T he mind is a very powerful part of a person's being. So the
apostle Paul, writer of Romans, said that in order for a person's life to be transformed, there must be a renewal of the mind.
By 'transformed' we mean a change from old to new, from failure
to success, from negative thinking to positive thinking.

YOUR MIND IS A GIFT

Your mind is a great gift. It is where your thoughts begin, and
from those thoughts arise your actions and behaviour. James Allen,
an inspirational writer, describes our thoughts as 'the silent forces
that can become beneficial when rightly directed, or destructive
when wrongly directed.' Your mind is powerful. Be careful what
thoughts you allow to dominate your thinking.

Proverbs 23:7 states, 'For as he thinks in his heart, so he is.' If you keep telling yourself that you are a failure, you will end up a failure because you'll start to believe your untamed thoughts!

No wonder Nikos Kazantzakis, a Greek writer, poet, and philosopher said, 'In order to succeed, we must first believe that we can.' Believing in yourself is half the battle.

CREATION BEGINS IN THE MIND

Ideas start in the mind before they take physical shape. Artists create a mental picture before they start to draw. When their actual drawing is not what they can see in their mind's eye, they erase it again and again until they get the picture they want. So it is for you. Your actions spring from what you have conceived in your mind.

The universe was created out of the thoughts of the Creator Himself. God knew how He wanted the heavens and earth to look before He began to create. Thus, at the end of creation, everything fitted His plan, He said everything 'was good' (Genesis 1:31). You have the ability to create with your minds through your thoughts, too.

POSITIVE AGAINST NEGATIVE THOUGHTS

As a human being, you are said to have on average 70,000 thoughts per day, which is approximately 3,000 thoughts per hour. Imagine what your life would be like if even 20 percent of your thoughts were negative. Pretty damaging!

You can dwell on positive thoughts, motivating yourself to take actions that will yield good results. Or you can dwell on negative thoughts and subject yourself to fear, worry and doubt.

Allowing negatives to dominate your thinking is like living in bondage. Good and positive thoughts are locked out of your life, because you spend the whole time processing negative thoughts, and never allowing a change in your thought processes.

When I was at university, I had a friend whose family was poor, and from time to time he would say, 'I am going to be successful and wealthy in life'. Everything around him indicated the opposite but years later, he is indeed living as a successful and wealthy man, with multiple businesses. The difference between my friend and a lot of people from the same background is that he allowed positive thoughts to control the steps he took. Your positive thoughts and choices will walk hand in hand to deliver a positive outcome. One without the other just doesn't work!

Now, this friend of mine was careful about what he allowed to dominate his thinking. Every time reality set in to remind him that his father was the poorest man in town, and that no other person in his family amounted to anything good in life, my friend would neutralise those thoughts of failure that wanted to enslave him, and begin to pull back the picture of what he wanted to become. And that made him jump into action by studying as hard as the task required.

We all have moments when negative thoughts creep in, but we can draw from the well of positive thinking and truths. Refuse to be enslaved by negative thinking!

You can create your own well of positive thinking by:

- reading your Bible, because that is where you develop the faith that can transform your thinking (Romans 10:17)
- surrounding yourself with positive-thinking people or resources, such as sound preachers of the gospel, books, educative television programmes and online resources

Napoleon Hill, the great writer, said, 'Whatever the mind can conceive and believe, it can achieve.' Success in life starts from your mind. The journey from teen to palace starts from the mind.

Proverbs 4:23 instructs us to 'above all else, guard your heart, for therein is the source of life.' In another Bible translation it says, '...for everything you do flows from it.' It means we must be mindful of what we allow to dominate our thinking. The opposite of life is death, therefore if the source of life is from a guarded heart, the source of death can be from an unguarded heart.

If you think constantly about negative things, you will start to believe them. Hope will ebb away. But when you spend your time thinking about good and positive things, there will be that inner urge to do what it takes to realise those positive thoughts.

YOUR THOUGHTS FORM YOUR HABITS

A friend once told me this: 'Your thinking creates your ideology. Your ideology creates your choices. Your choices shape your actions. Your actions determine your habits. Your habits determine your lifestyle. Your lifestyle determines your destiny.'

Wow!

Habits are behaviours we repeatedly do. They can have an effect on the person you become. If you have the habit of indulging in junk food, sooner or later it will tell on your health. Procrastination – the habit of constantly putting off doing something –means you may never realise your dreams if you never get around to taking action.

Are you in danger of throwing away your potential because of bad habits? I mentor a young lady called Lauren who is 23 years of age. She expresses such regret at the effect her teenage behaviour has had (and continues to have) on her life. She behaved so badly at school, did not listen to her teachers nor even her mum. Now she's unqualified and can't hold down a job, she's restless, she has no focus. She just wishes she had heard and acted on good advice when she was younger.

A young man I know steals from his mum's purse. He thinks it's fine if she doesn't find out. But whether she finds out or not, it's wrong. And it's establishing a habit that may land him in prison one day.

The earlier you can recognise your bad habits and reject them, the easier it is to change your ways. Where will they lead you otherwise? It's never too late to make a fresh start and win back your future.

Discipline yourself to resist habits that may defer (or even ruin) your dream future. Jim Rohn, the motivational speaker, said, 'Discipline is the bridge between goals and accomplishment.' To get to your palace, you have to be disciplined in the way you behave.

FAITH AND THINKING

The writer of Hebrews defines faith as 'the way of holding onto what we hope for, being certain of what we cannot see.' (Hebrews 11:1) In effect, you must believe that you are capable of attaining goals with the help of God.

Take the risk of believing in the big dream you have! Your positivity and God's grace are an amazing combination!

45

Accept that nothing is impossible for God (Matthew 19: 26). Take the risk of believing in the big dream you have! Your positivity and God's grace are an amazing combination!

YOUR DREAMS AND YOUR MIND

A lot of people have dreams that die with them. For a dream to be achieved, it must pass through a thought process until it is clear what must be done to bring it to pass. Negative thoughts must be overcome.

I once watched an inspiring film called 'The Ultimate Gift'. In it, a little girl called Emily asks Jason, an older man, if he has a dream. At the time, Jason hadn't figured out what it was to have a dream, but when he did, nothing could stop the lengths he was ready to go to in order to fulfil this dream! He found solutions to everything that posed a challenge. His thinking was transformed! Are you like Jason? Why not look for your dream?

Joseph, the man we read about in the Bible with a gift for interpreting dreams, (Genesis 39:19-21), was put in prison for a crime he did not commit. He had the option to dwell on the consequences of his punishment (death) and live in fear. But instead, I believe he chose to remember and dwell on the thoughts of the dream he had as a teenager, that one day, his father and brothers (Genesis 37:9) were going to bow down to him. I can almost hear him saying, 'The palace is my final destination. I will be a prime minister one day. This is not the end of my life. Even if everybody in this prison is killed, I am coming out alive, I will see my father and brothers again, and they will bow down to me according to the dreams God showed me.'

Let the dream God has shown you dominate your thoughts. If you understand what the seed of greatness in you represents, that should be the paramount thing to pursue.

> *Let the dream God has shown you dominate your thoughts.*

But listen up! This doesn't mean that you can ignore your other responsibilities or drop out of school to follow a dream! We can't expect everything to fall into place this very minute. But hold fast to your aspirations; plan to attain them at the right time. You hold the key to your future.

> *This doesn't mean that you can ignore your other responsibilities or drop out of school to follow a dream!*

PRACTICAL STEPS TO DEVELOP YOUR THINKING

Some practical steps you can take to develop or improve your thinking are:

- Always remember who you are; made in the image and likeness of God.
- Have a dream for your life and a practical, wise plan of how to pursue it.
- Don't be a slave to negative thoughts. Eleanor Roosevelt said, 'No one can make you feel inferior without your consent.'
- Think and speak positively to yourself.
- Be influenced by wise, positive role models.

- Study and engage with the truth of Scriptures.
- Pray for a renewal of mind. This can be a world-changer! Do not have a closed heart that harbours negativity only.
- Read good, motivational books.
- Listen to the teachings and preachings of Godly people.
- Pray for the Holy Spirit to guard your heart always.
- Follow the practical principles in this book!

You have the power to choose what consumes your thoughts. The best thing that you can do right now is to learn to dwell on positive thoughts alone. Living in the palace requires you to transform your thinking and guard your heart with diligence.

'If you can dream it, you can do it'–Walt Disney

APPLICATION

Before you move on, why not take a pen and notepad and write down those areas of your life where your thoughts have held you bound, and begin to follow the steps above to undo them?

CHAPTER 3

PLAN FOR INTENTIONAL GROWTH

———⟨❈⟩———

'You will never change your life until you change
something you do daily.'

–John C. Maxwell

A lot of people believe that getting to the palace is a matter of luck. This is not the case! A few people may be blessed in this way by being in the right place at the right time, or meeting those who can and do help them. But for the vast majority, getting to their palace will require intentional growth and action, without which they may never achieve their dreams.

HOW WE GROW

Growth is the process of increasing in size, such as the development from childhood to adulthood. Intentional growth is that which is intended, done on purpose: planned steps you can take towards your upward movement towards a desired result.

When you plant a seed in summer and don't water it, it doesn't thrive; it could die because it isn't getting what it needs. An intentional decision to provide water is necessary for the desired outcome.

> *Growth does not just happen by chance. It must be intentional. A baby that is not well fed will not grow; it may even die of malnutrition.*

The same goes for a person who wants to reach the palace. Growth does not just happen by chance. It must be intentional. A baby that is not well fed will not grow; it may even die of malnutrition.

This intentional growth can make all the difference between those who end up in their palace and others who end up in a life of mediocrity or regret.

People who are intentional about their growth are those who brainstorm and plan how to make positive changes in their life; they work hard to achieve the skills they lack; they do whatever it takes (within the law!) to get to where they ought to be in life.

The difference between the teens who spend extra time preparing for their exams and those who can't be bothered, is intentional growth. For you to move from teen to palace, a plan for intentional growth must be in place from now.

INTENTIONAL GROWTH NEEDS DETERMINATION!

You may see some obstacles to making changes in your life. What if your parents are not supportive? What if you do not believe in yourself? What if there's no-one to help? What if you don't know where to start? What if you do not have the resources to start?

There is always some positive step you can take. Yes, there are obstacles. For some people, there are very great obstacles. But don't allow your obstacles to become excuses that make you think change is impossible for you. Don't be a slave to negative thoughts! Start with small steps, small goals. Small victories will encourage you to keep striving.

Success will not just fall into your lap. Be determined to stick to a growth plan that will get you there. Look for people who have done what you want to do, and emulate them. When disappointments and failures come, accept them as part of the journey and learn from them.

When disappointments and failures come, accept them as part of the journey and learn from them.

When you are aspiring to move from teen to palace, here are some of the questions you need to answer to help you achieve intentional growth:

- Who am I?
- Why am I here on earth?

- What do I want to become in the future?
- How far can I go in my dreams and aspirations?
- Where and how do I start?
- What sort of lifestyle should I expose myself to?
- Who are my mentors and role models?
- Who are my friends, confidants, and advisers?

'I am just thirteen, how can I know the answers to these questions?'

'But I have nobody to teach me.'

Well, the good news is that you are reading this book now. It is not too late to start answering these questions and putting in place the right measures to help you in your growth.

START TODAY

Tomorrow is not the best time to start. You have to start now. Right now! Get a head start by engaging your mind in positive thinking, drawing a mind map (more about this in the next chapter!), having a photo of where you want to be in a place where you can see it all the time, dreaming the big dreams and seeing yourself seated in the palace you desire. Do not procrastinate. Procrastination is said to be the thief of time, and it is certainly a dream killer.

I remember countless times talking to young people when the question pops up: 'What do you want to be when you're older?' And you hear some saying, 'I don't know, I've not even thought about it, I don't really want to become anything.' Only about three percent give positive answers.

As a teen there is no need to put pressure on yourself to have your whole future planned out already. Just make sure that you focus on developing yourself, making the best of your gifts and abilities in life so that many opportunities will be open to you as you get older.

You have what it takes, the seed of greatness is inside of you. You may not find out for a while what your seed is, but without doubt you are fearfully and wonderfully made (Psalm 139:14)–so start expecting a great future! Benjamin Franklin, one of the Founding Fathers of the United States once said, 'By failing to prepare, you are preparing to fail.'

The Bible says in Ecclesiastes 3:1-8, 'For everything, there is a season and a time for....' A time to plant and a time to reap, whether good or bad. Don't miss any opportunity, don't settle for less than you desire or deserve.

Recognising that change is needed and taking gradual steps to alter your path is the best way to go about it.

INTENTIONAL GROWTH IS NOT DRASTIC

Planning your growth does not mean a drastic shift from where you are now if you have found yourself going in the wrong direction in life. It means being aware that you are heading in the wrong direction, and making the decision to change your values, habits and everything else holding you in that position. Making dramatic changes without a well thought-out plan may make things worse if you act irrationally.

Recognising that change is needed and taking gradual steps to alter your path is the best way to go about it. For example, try to get more sleep, don't join the group of friends who are bunking classes, avoid smoking or drinking alcohol, try to respect your teachers and steer clear of those who are breaking the law. Intentionally avoid the things that are going to hold you back from fulfilling your amazing potential.

INTENTIONAL GROWTH HELPS YOU STAY ON TRACK

When I was growing up, there was a cool kid in my neighbourhood who everyone looked up to. He was good looking, brainy and popular. But by the time he was 14, he had started smoking. From regular cigarettes he grew quickly into using drugs. By Year 10, he dropped out of school as a result of mental illness.

I heard of another young girl who used to sneak out of school to be with her boyfriend. Before anyone had a chance to deal with her truanting, she was pregnant and became a mum at the age of fifteen. That was the end of her education.

But without an intentional plan to stick on the right path, it's very easy to lose your way.

These are young people who had a bright future but drifted unintentionally into habits that had a serious impact on their future. They didn't plan for things to go wrong, but without an intentional plan to stick on the right path, it's very easy to lose your way. A lot of teenagers fall victim to damaging lifestyles and bad company at some point. All these can be avoided as a teenager when you are intentional about your growth.

The stories of the young men who became presidents of nations like the United States tell of how they worked tirelessly for this dream. Whether

> *Whether you plan to be a president of your country or to run an international charity, it all needs an intentional growth plan.*

you plan to be a president of your country or to run an international charity, it all needs an intentional growth plan.

SOME PARENTS ARE INTENTIONAL ABOUT THEIR CHILDREN'S GROWTH

I once had a chat with a guy called Ken. He wasn't wealthy but he managed to get his three children through private education. Asked how he managed it, he replied, 'Marina, with the help of God, my wife and I sat down to plan the number of children we wanted. We wrote down the schools we wanted them to attend and began to save up even before our first was born. We never had holidays outside the UK, and drove a rickety old car until our last child finished secondary school. We wanted to give our children the education that our parents could not afford for us.'

> *Success is not accidental.*

The principle to take from Ken's story is that success is not accidental. Ken and his wife intentionally planned for the growth of their children. You may not have a father like Ken, but you can still do your best from where you are now, by intentionally planning.

9 STEPS FOR INTENTIONAL GROWTH

1   Apply all the steps in the other chapters of this book.

2   Take time to educate yourself. You can't just depend on what you learn in the classroom. Read biographies, do further study, and research your dreams. Nelson Mandela said, 'There is no passion to be found playing small, in settling for a life that is less than the one you are capable of living.'

3   Ask questions of those who have done what you intend to do.

4   Get a mentor. A friend, a family member, an employer. It is very beneficial to learn from other people's experience and mistakes.

5   Don't ask a pessimist for advice! You will get discouraged. The philosopher Epictetus said, 'The key is to keep company with people who uplift you, whose presence calls forth your best.'

6   Stay focused and motivated. Let your dreams be your driving force.

Stay focused and motivated. Let your dreams be your driving force

7   Save what you can for the future, should you need to buy something to help you achieve your dream.

8   Intentional growth can apply to any area of your life: finance, education, career. Set goals for all of them and take action.

9   Always commit your plans to God for His guidance and approval. Without Him, you can do nothing (John 15:5)

APPLICATION

Wait a second! Are there areas in your life where you need growth? Why not write them out and draw up the plans that will help you grow? Your life will never be the same again.

CHAPTER 4

SET GOALS IN YOUR LIFE

———⌒✦⌒———

'A goal is a dream with a deadline.'–Napoleon Hill

WHAT IS GOAL SETTING?

A goal is your aim in life, whether it concerns your career, education, sport or personal development. To achieve any goal, a plan must be made and actions taken on a day-to-day basis. This process is known as goal-setting. And it's never too early to start!

Many people today don't have a clear idea of what they want to achieve so they don't set goals. There are also a great many people who do have an idea, but don't know how to set goals. Some others believe that goal-setting is only necessary when you are facing a big project such as getting married. They forget that becoming successful in life is a big project, and as such will require well-defined goals from the start!

WHY SET GOAL?

Having goals gives you purpose; helps you take control of your life; informs your decisions; helps you stay focused; gives you a sense of direction; saves you time and money; and gives you fulfilment and something to strive for.

Sounds good? So here's how to go about it.

6 STEPS TO SETTING AND ACHIEVING THE RIGHT GOALS

1   DECIDE YOUR GOALS

Take a sheet of paper and write down all you want to be, do and have in life. Write as many things as possible.

Looking at your list, begin to sift out those things you know are not important. If you find this difficult, rate them on a scale of 1 to 10, and get rid of those things that score less than 8. Or look at your motives. For example, if you want to buy a new bike because your friend just bought one, you may realise that's not a good enough reason for you to get one.

You may wish to group your list into key areas such as personal, family, religious, study, career, sport or hobbies.

2   BREAK EACH GOAL DOWN

Carefully breaking your goals down into smaller parts will make them seem less daunting. Abraham Lincoln said that 'the best thing about the future is that it comes only one day at a time.' Taking small daily steps is all that's needed to turn your dreams into reality. Ask any marathon runner: before training, they could probably only run for 30 seconds! And that is a great achievement on day one!

Some goals may require more help or effort. Breaking down your goals will give you an idea of what costs may be involved (in time, money or effort), what obstacles you may encounter, and what things you will need to avoid to achieve your dream. You'll need to be aware of the kind of company to keep, the kind of thoughts to dwell on.

It may help to consider how much time you want to spend on different areas of your life every day or every week: socialising, sport, study. Then you can plan when to get things done and they're more likely to happen. So much becomes achievable when thought out and written down.

Make a to-do list for each day with small, achievable tasks. Cross them off when you're done, then focus on new ones. You'll be able to see the progress you're making. Reward yourself for your achievements.

3   WRITE YOUR GOALS DOWN AND DISPLAY THEM

Goal-setting is recommended in the Bible. In Habakkuk 2:2-3 we read, 'Write the vision down, inscribe it on tablets to be easily read. For the vision is for its appointed time, it hastens towards its end and it will not lie; although it may take some time, wait for it, for come it certainly will before too long.'

This scripture is encouraging you to write down your goals where you can see them as a constant reminder and encouragement. Expressing your goal in writing brings clarity to your vision. If you don't commit your plans to paper, there is a tendency to forget and even abandon them, because we humans are easily distracted and discouraged.

You may prefer to create a vision board, where you display pictures of what you want to become or achieve in life. Every time you walk past it, it reminds you of what you are walking towards.

Whether in words or pictures, look at your goals and dreams daily. Remind yourself why and how you need to achieve them. This will drive out the negativity that grips us all from time to time.

CASE STUDY

Anita was 16 when she took steps to pursue her dream of becoming a doctor. All her friends chose arts and language subjects at college, but Anita opted for sciences. She misses being with her friends in class, but her dream is too precious to sacrifice. When asked how she became so determined, she says that when she turned 14, her parents sat her down and helped her draw a vision board around her dream. When she woke up every morning, this vision board was staring at her and she knew how to make it become reality.

It was meeting her Uncle Dan and hearing about his job as a doctor that first sparked the dream. She was just a child but, she says, 'we bonded so well, we had a lot in common, we are both so passionate about people's wellbeing, and I found myself always asking him questions about his job. One day, I went to his surgery. I sat on his chair, had his stethoscope around my neck and was immediately in love with the career. On returning home, I began to tell everyone that when I grew up, I'd be a doctor. I have had a lot of support from everyone since that pronouncement, and every Christmas my Uncle Dan bought me a gift that would remind me of my dream career, to help keep the dream alive. Mum and Dad helping me with the vision board has made everything simpler and clearer for me.'

Anita got support from her family. You can also get support from your family, teachers, pastors or church leaders, mentors, coaches and people who have done and succeeded in what you want to do.

4   PURSUE YOUR GOALS IN ORDER OF PRIORITY

Don't try to pursue many goals at the same time. If you are over-ambitious, you are more likely to fail and become discouraged. Take one at a time, broken down into manageable steps and in order of priority.

It may help if you consider which of your goals are

- ongoing (such as getting to school on time)
- short-term (something to do in the next week or two)
- medium-term (things for the next year)
- long-term (these goals may take many years to achieve)

Let's take Anna as an example. She's a Year 12 student who has identified three goals to achieve in the next two years:

- To get into university.
- To learn how to drive and buy a car.
- To learn a second language.

Her priority must be her final exams, which will come around in a few months. She therefore, has an automatic deadline imposed on her. Success in these exams is the key to university. She will need to be committed to studying, to getting enough sleep, to limiting her social life and other commitments, to having a revision plan.

Learning to drive cannot be started until she is 17 years old. In the mean time, she could save some money to pay for driving lessons, consider getting a part-time job to fund them. By researching the cost, she can make a realistic plan of when this is achievable. She needs also to consider whether she can borrow her parents' car to practise, as this will make the process quicker. Once she is at university, access to a car may be harder, in which case her deadline should be based around the availability of the car.

By researching the cost, she can make a realistic plan of when this is achievable.

Learning a language can be done at college or online. It could even be offered as an additional course at the university she goes to. This goal is more flexible, but she will still need to set the time she aims to achieve it. She can research her options and fit it in at a suitable time.

5   ALLOCATE A TIMESCALE

Give yourself a realistic deadline. It'll gear you into action! Think about how long it may take you to achieve each step towards your goal; write it down as it will help to motivate you and keep your focus. Without a timescale you are likely to lose motivation.

6   PRAY

Ask God to help you find your unique path in life. Always remember to pray about your goals every day. No matter how enthusiastic and committed you are, only God can give you the grace to succeed and grant you peace in your career.

Lastly, remember your goals should be **SMART**:

- Specific –identify the specific area of your goal.
- Measurable – have a plan in place, so you know whether you are progressing or not.
- Achievable – think practically. You can't expect to pass an exam without sufficient time and preparation.
- Realistic – there are no short cuts. You can't be a surgeon next year when you have not even started university yet. Success won't happen overnight.
- Time-bound – give yourself a deadline to work towards.

Remember that goal-setting is there to help you live your life to the full and achieve what you are capable of achieving. It's not about regimenting your life with rules at every turn. Don't be too hard on yourself. Accept your mistakes and celebrate your successes.

It's your turn!

Take five minutes to jot down some ideas that came to you while you read this chapter.

What are your dreams, big or small? Is there anything you need to do right now but keep putting off? Are there things you want to do now, but you aren't sure how to achieve them? Where would you like to be in five, ten or twenty years' time? What would you aim for if you knew you couldn't fail? Remember, well-set goals are a step towards your palace.

Go for it!

CHAPTER 5

MAKE THE RIGHT CHOICES

—⚬⚬❖⚬⚬—

'One's philosophy is not best expressed in words;
it is expressed in the choices one makes... and the
choices we make are ultimately our responsibility.'-
Eleanor Roosevelt

WHAT ARE CHOICES?

Wikipedia says that 'choice involves mentally making a decision: judging the merits of multiple options and selecting one or more of them. One can make a choice between imagined options or between real options'. And the online dictionary defines choice as 'an act of choosing between two or more possibilities.' Simply put, choice involves decision-making, either between good and evil, or between good, better and best.

> *Choice involves decision-making, either between good and evil, or between good, better and best.*

Choices are like roads leading to different destinations: the one you take determines where you end up. And which road you choose depends on your values and beliefs.

Choices have consequences. Some good, some bad. They all shape the world you live in.

YOUR CHOICES CAN MAKE OR BREAK YOU

Right choices are the quickest route to your palace.

Life is full of choices, just as living in the palace is a choice. It is important that from an early age, you learn to make the right choices. Right choices are the quickest route to your palace.

One day I was having a conversation with my husband, and we wondered why some Christians seem to have a smooth life: they marry at the right time, have a good job and seem not to have problems! As we deliberated on it and considered the lives of a few friends, it came to us that what these people have in common is that they gave their lives to Christ as teenagers and chose to follow through with what they believed.

The teachings of the Bible were their standard for living. They never turned back from what they knew as Christians, and, because God is true to His promises, He has been faithful to them. Following the teachings of the Bible does not mean they were fanatics or spent their whole life praying. They just took the required steps to get them to their palaces.

And then we have those who had the opportunity of hearing the same gospel, but chose to be in church one day, and continue with bad habits the next, habits which were an offence to God and could not lead to fulfilment. And today, their lives bear witness to those wrong choices.

THE CONSEQUENCES OF YOUR CHOICES

Making the wrong choice can have an impact on others, even the next generation. For instance, the Bible advises us to refrain from sex before marriage,

Making the wrong choice can have an impact on others, even the next generation.

because it is a valuable gift not to be thrown away lightly. It carries great consequences, spiritually, emotionally and physically.

Think about these things. You do have a choice. Many teenagers suddenly find themselves in situations they never imagined could happen, all because of a spur-of-the-moment choice.

Sexually transmitted diseases are at epidemic levels. And unplanned teenage pregnancy is common. Many teens choose to have an abortion, saying that they are too young to be parents; they want to enjoy their lives and so on. They forget that they don't own their lives, and if their mum had aborted them, they would not be alive!

Others are persuaded to terminate the pregnancy by their parents, nurse or boyfriend. But abortion is not a 'quick fix'; it cuts short a new life and causes terrible emotional damage to the mother.

And it has an impact on the world, too. You never know who an unborn child will become, what potential they have, how many lives they may touch.

You never know who an unborn child will become, what potential they have, how many lives they may touch.

Some do decide to keep the baby. It's a brave decision and these girls are to be supported. But it involves sacrifice. Having a baby as a teenager is not the ideal time.

It takes just a second to make a choice that can have consequences for a lifetime. And many young people today make these choices because of peer pressure and lack of sound advice. They end up doing things that could hurt them for years to come.

Breaking the law, being kicked out of school, sleeping around, trying drugs 'just once'... these things take you down a road leading to a destination you'll regret. And it's certainly not a destination where you can reach your full potential in life.

We read the story of Esau in Genesis 25:29-34. When he was hungry, he wanted his brother, Jacob's meal. But Jacob would only give it to him in return for Esau's special rights as firstborn son. Esau had the choice not to sell his birthright for a meal, but he chose to do so. He didn't think it would matter, but it brought greater consequences for him. Jacob later got the firstborn blessing that was meant for Esau as a result of his wrong choice earlier on.

It's important to remember that everyone makes bad choices at some point. Don't beat yourself up over past mistakes. Learn from them and remember that with God you can always seek forgiveness and a new start.

LET NOTHING STOP YOU FROM MAKING GOOD CHOICES

Some people know what they want in life, but they hold back from making the necessary choices because they only focus on their limitations.

I read an article about a young man named Bradley Warwick from Bristol. Bradley was 21 years old, severely disabled with cerebral palsy, and he had just joined an orchestra. He was to play ground bass for the South West Open Youth Orchestra, using only his eyes and some clever software called EyeKeys that detected which notes he was looking at. This story inspired me because I could see that Bradley's disability did not hold him back; he just found a way around it!

CHOOSE TO TAKE RESPONSIBILITY

We would all love to be whisked to a palace, to enjoy the benefits without the hard work. But as Gordon B. Hinckley put it, 'Without hard work, nothing grows but weeds.'

Don't wait until you're shoulder-high in weeds, miles from your palace, then lay the blame on your parents and your surroundings.

The Oscar-winning actress Katharine Hepburn said, 'We are taught you must blame your father, your sisters, your brothers, the school, the teachers–but never blame yourself. It's never your fault. But it's always your fault, because if you wanted to change you're the one who has got to change.'

But don't feel you're facing it alone! You may need some help making certain decisions. It can be very hard to work things out alone. Speaking to someone you trust and admire is a good start. And don't feel you have to rush into big decisions; with time the answer often becomes clear.

YOUR CHOICES ARE TIED TO YOUR DESTINY

*To make the wrong choice is to forget your assignment.
It is to forget that you have a great purpose, and
your choices are what will get you there.*

A university student on his twenty-first birthday, dared by his friend, chose to drink over his limit and died of alcohol poisoning. His destiny was cut short by a moment of madness, his friend's life ruined too.

In the Bible, we read about how Joshua understood this (Joshua 24:14-15). He told the children of Israel–who at the time worshipped idols–to choose whom they would serve. He proclaimed that he and his family would serve the Lord. What wisdom! He knew that his help was from God and he was not ready for the people to lead him astray by their wrong choice. Not everyone gets the opportunity to be led by a good leader like Joshua. So make a choice about where you stand today; stay away from people that will lead you down the wrong path.

Technology can be of benefit and harm to you. Using technology wisely is using time wisely. Youngsters stay on social media more than they do anything else. An article in the Metro by Harry Readhead reported that children who spend more than three hours a day on social media sites are twice as likely to have mental health issues. The ONS report he quotes found higher levels of emotional problems, social issues, hyperactivity, and poor behaviour among youngsters who spent long periods of time on sites like Facebook, Twitter or Instagram.

Using technology wisely is using time wisely.

What choices are you making?
Think about how they could affect your destiny.

HOW TO MAKE GOOD CHOICES

Bobby Knight, a retired American basketball coach, said, "The will to succeed is important, but what's more important is the will to prepare." Prepare for success by making wise, brave choices.

Prepare for success by making wise, brave choices.

Some choices are not between good and bad, but between two good outcomes! Weigh up which will be of greatest benefit to you and others.

SOME PRACTICAL STEPS TO CONSIDER IN YOUR CHOICE-MAKING:

1 Be clear about exactly what choice you are facing and the possible options.

2 Seek advice from people who have been in a similar situation. Remember; do not go to the pessimists!

3 Weigh the good and bad consequences of making each choice. Think of the longer term impacts, not just the instant rewards.

4 Pray about it and let God direct you in making the best choice on the issue.

5 Take action.

Remember that good choices don't always feel good.
Sometimes they require courage and going against what your friends are doing, being laughed at even.

But the important thing is to choose to do the right thing. In this way, you will grow in strength.

Make the right choices today; you will build a great future!

APPLICATION

Are there areas in your life where you are struggling to make good choices, or are you currently suffering from the effect of a wrong choice you made? It's not too late; take a sheet of paper and write out the areas of your life where you need to make a choice. Follow the steps and take action.

CHAPTER 6

SEEK KNOWLEDGE

———⚬✧⚬———

'Learning is the beginning of wealth. Learning is
the beginning of health. Learning is the beginning
of spirituality. Searching and learning is where the
miracle process all begins.'

–Jim Rohn

WHAT IS KNOWLEDGE?

The online dictionary defines knowledge as 'facts, information and skills acquired through experience or education.' We all need knowledge to move from where we are to where we need to be.

Ignorance is the opposite of knowledge; it is very dangerous. It can lead people blindly into trouble and hold them back from getting to their palaces.

Ignorance is the opposite of knowledge; it is very dangerous. It can lead people blindly into trouble and hold them back from getting to their palaces. Even seemingly small things, like eating the wrong foods because you don't understand the effect on your body, can have negative consequences.

If you need to know something that could improve your life but are not doing anything to gain that knowledge, you will be left behind. Others will be climbing on the ladder of success as a result of what they know.

As a teen aspiring to palace life, gaining the right knowledge is the best thing that you can do. In the Bible, the prophet Hosea writes, 'My people are destroyed for lack of knowledge.' (Hosea 4:6). Those who do not seek knowledge are at a disadvantage.

Learning is the starting point of every good thing: health, spirituality, relationships, financial management, skill, the list could go on and on. Where and how can we learn?

WHERE TO ACQUIRE KNOWLEDGE

Knowledge can be gained in various areas. You may struggle at school, but you can still become the person God wants you to be. Read on!

1   EDUCATION

Nelson Mandela, former President of South Africa, said, 'Education is the most powerful weapon which you can use to change the world.' Those who make it from teen to palace can change their world.

Education can be formal or informal. Formal education can be undertaken at school, by home schooling or by distance/online learning. Through formal education, you learn to read, write and acquire basic skills. There is a structured curriculum to be followed from nursery through to university. Formal education is the most popular form of education as it is encouraged (and enforced to a certain level) by the governments of both developed and developing nations of the world. A certificate acquired from formal education in one country is accepted in most other countries worldwide.

Formal education can give people the knowledge and tools to improve their country and economy; reduce poverty; increase their own income; access facts and information; gain social skills to fit into society; establish global connections, increase self-confidence and many more.

Formal education may not bring everyone success or to the palace but it does for the vast majority of people. It opens doors to certain careers. I hear a lot of teenagers say school is boring but if you aspire to live a palace life, you may want to be different and say yes to formal education, keeping in mind the long-term benefits. Aristotle said, 'The roots of education are bitter, but the fruit is sweet.'

Self-education is an example of informal education. It is when you acquire knowledge through personal study. Its advantages are

When you acquire knowledge through personal study. that you can expand on areas of particular interest to you or acquire knowledge which may not be taught during formal education, such as learning more about God and His principles, money management, living a life of purpose and so on. As Haruki Murakami, a Japanese writer, said, 'If you only read the books that everyone else is reading, you can only think what everyone is thinking.'

Self-education certainly opens golden doors, because you learn more than your contemporaries. You have a vast knowledge in areas they have never ventured into, which gives you great confidence and an edge over a wide range of people. When you have a great passion to learn, you never stop growing.

You may wonder where to start. Find good materials and books. The younger you start, the better. Start by reading books meant for your age group in an area of interest to you. Or biographies of people you admire. Try your local library, it's free to join. There are great resources out there to motivate you. Do something starting today, no matter how small. Make a goal to read at least six books a year that will add value to your life.

2   KNOWLEDGE FROM GOD

One of the best books to read as a teen is your Bible. Read it from start to finish, Genesis to Revelation, twice

One of the best books to read as a teen is your Bible.

through your teenage years if possible. This will help your brain grow more than anything else. It will be the secret behind your excellence in life because all the wisdom you need to run your life is embedded in the Bible.

God is the greatest giver of knowledge, acquired through His Word.

We can gain great knowledge when we study our Bible. We learn how to relate with God and our fellow humans. God is the greatest giver of knowledge, acquired through His Word. In Daniel 1:17, it states, 'As for these four youths, God gave them knowledge and intelligence in every branch of literature and wisdom; Daniel even understood all kinds of visions and dreams.'

God can give knowledge to you too, but you will need a deep relationship with Him and to walk in His ways like Daniel did.

3   LEARNING FROM OTHERS

Learn from those people who are doing what you want to do: your boss, your neighbour, your family, your mentor, your teacher, your pastor, or through specific TV shows in areas that are helpful. This knowledge can come from an apprenticeship, simply by asking questions or just by watching the way people you admire do things. There are people with a wealth of experience and expertise to share with you. They can help you to solve difficult problems or make the most of your life. You'll find most people are pleased to be asked for their advice! Who knows how they might help you!

4   MIX WITH THE RIGHT PEOPLE

This is usually the easiest way to seek knowledge. It can be in group settings, like when you go to your friend's house and are part of their family discussions. Sometimes just overhearing other conversations, even if you are not joining in, can be useful.

Just remember to learn from people you look up to and trust. Some advice is misleading.

BEWARE OF FALSE KNOWLEDGE

George Bernard Shaw, the Irish playwright, warns us to 'Beware of false knowledge; it is more dangerous than ignorance.'

False knowledge is when we learn something that is in fact wrong. This is worse than having no knowledge at all! Be thorough in whatever field you delve into; learn from reliable sources. Don't accept that everything you read or hear is true or the right road to take.

Remember that after discovering your seed of greatness, you must nurture and protect it. For this you must seek good knowledge, and avoid being misled. For False knowledge is worse than ignorance.

Pray for God to give you wisdom and understanding.

APPLICATION

How much knowledge do you have and how much knowledge are you looking to acquire? Have you been wondering how to move from teen to palace but have limited knowledge? Look at where you are now, follow the steps above for acquiring knowledge, and take action.

CHAPTER 7

GROWING IN WISDOM

———— ∽❦∾ ————

'For wisdom is far more valuable than rubies.
Nothing you desire can compare with it.'

–Proverbs 8:11

When I started writing this chapter, my husband saw the title and said, 'I thought your last chapter was on knowledge? You should have written about wisdom in there because they go together. Why have a separate chapter on wisdom?'

Well, I managed to make him see why! I think you will too by the end of this chapter.

WHAT IS WISDOM?

Wisdom is the display of sound judgment, 'the application of knowledge', the ability to judge right from wrong, the natural ability to understand and apply what others do not understand, to act with discretion and prudence. The word 'wisdom' appears over

230 times in the Bible!

Wisdom and knowledge are related, but they are not the same. The Bible talks about them both, as well as understanding. For you to be successful in life you need all three. You may have great knowledge and yet not

You may have great knowledge and yet not have wisdom. (The opposite of wisdom is foolishness. And some very clever people are foolish!)

have wisdom. (The opposite of wisdom is foolishness. And some very clever people are foolish!)

Consider a brain surgeon: he has studied for years to acquire great medical knowledge and skill. One night he drinks too much alcohol at a party and decides to drive home. He thinks he'll get away with it and can't be bothered to call for a taxi. He risks causing an accident, hurting someone, losing his licence, his reputation and even his job. Very unwise.

Similarly, there may be a kid you know at school who is bottom of every class. He is never going to pass his exams; he just finds the work too hard. But he knows to avoid hanging out with the bad crowd. He has seen his uncle go to prison for theft and he is determined to stay out of trouble, even if he's tempted. That's a wise kid.

It takes wisdom to choose the right course or career

Some of you reading this may go to college or university. There, you will acquire more knowledge. But it takes wisdom to choose the right course or career in the first place, so that you can make the most of the educational opportunities available to you.

SOURCES OF WISDOM

There are two kinds of wisdom: secular (or worldly) wisdom, and supernatural (or divine) wisdom. They can be found in the following:

1   EXPERIENCE

Learn from your own or others' experiences. It's not enough just to know what happened; you must use that knowledge to make decisions in the future.

2   ADVICES FROM OTHERS

In the Book of Proverbs, we read that '...wisdom is found in those who take advice' (13:10). Some older people especially have very wise advice to pass on; they have learnt from a lifetime of good and bad experience.

3   GROWTH AND DEVELOPMENT THAT COME WITH AGE

You can't have great wisdom on day one. We read in the Bible that even Jesus grew in wisdom throughout his childhood and teenage years.

4 WISDOM FROM GOD

True wisdom, which is divine wisdom, is that which God alone can give. Wisdom from God is different from intelligence, smartness or having a high I.Q. It concerns moral, spiritual and religious values. It looks beyond the here and now to a greater place. It is different from what we call 'worldly wisdom' because the wisdom of this world often seeks power, wealth and temporary rewards, no matter the consequences for others.

Wisdom from God is different from intelligence, smartness or having a high I.Q. It concerns moral, spiritual and religious values.

DIVINE WISDOM

In the Book of Proverbs, we read that the man who finds wisdom is blessed; that is, not only happy, but fruitful in all His ways because true wisdom is God's wisdom (Proverbs 3:13).

While wisdom gained from the first three sources listed above are useful, they can be unreliable, relying as they do on humans, who are weak and sinful. The apostle Paul even goes so far as to say that 'the wisdom of this world is foolishness in God's eyes' (I Corinthians 3:19)!

wisdom acquired from God can take you from where you are to your palace.

But wisdom acquired from God can take you from where you are to your palace. King Solomon understood the essence and need for divine wisdom, hence he asked the Lord for it during his early days as a king of Israel.

9 WAYS IN WHICH GOD'S WISDOM IS WORTH MORE THAN GOLD:

1. It helps you to identify your seed of greatness and excel in all you do.
2. It helps you to make the right choices, whether for studies, jobs or relationships.
3. It keeps you safe, helping you discern between right and wrong.
4. It helps you reflect on your life and identify areas to improve.
5. It makes you stand out from the crowd.
6. It makes your day-to-day life easier and happier.
7. It teaches you how to know, love and fear God.
8. It leads to humility, respect, and service toward others. The Bible tells us that 'the wisdom which comes from above is pure and peace-loving. Persons with this wisdom show understanding and listen to advice; they are full of compassion and good works; they are impartial and sincere.' (James 3:17)
9. God created the universe by His wisdom, so you too can create because you are made in His image.

That is why Proverbs 3:13-18 states:

'Happy is the man who finds wisdom, and the man who gains understanding; for her proceeds are better than the profits of silver, and her gain than fine gold. She is more precious than rubies, and all the things you may desire cannot compare with her. Length of days is in her right hand, in her left hand riches and honour. Her ways are ways of pleasantness, and all her paths are peace. She is a tree of life to those who take hold of her, and happy are all who retain her.'

HOW TO OBTAIN DIVINE WISDOM

Proverbs 1:7 tells us that wisdom starts with the fear of the Lord. It's worth us taking a minute here to look at what this phrase means. The famous preacher Father Cantalamessa explained it like this:

It is born from knowledge of who God is.

'The fear of God is quite different from being afraid. The fear of God must be learned. It is born from knowledge of who God is. It is the same sentiment that we feel before some great spectacle of nature. It is feeling small before something that is immense; it is marvel mixed with admiration. This fear is often called 'the beginning of wisdom' because it leads to making the right choices in life.'

So the first thing is to acknowledge the greatness of God and our dependence on Him.

Second, we simply need to ask for divine wisdom! According to James 1:5, God gives wisdom to all who ask Him! For example, King Solomon (in 1 Kings 5:12) asked for wisdom, and God granted it to him. His gift of wisdom was tested when two women came to him to determine which of two babies (one alive, one dead) belonged to each of them. Can you image for a minute how he could have made that decision had God not given him the gift of wisdom? He would probably have made the wrong choice, persuaded by the more outspoken woman to hand her the living child.

Third: we can also grow in divine wisdom by reading the Bible. The Book of Proverbs is full of wisdom because it was written by Solomon, the wisest man who ever lived. If you study the Book of Proverbs, understand it and apply it to your life, you will find it a very practical help.

Fourth: prayer. Prayer is simply spending time with God, communicating with Him in our hearts, listening to Him, developing a relationship. The closer we get to Him, the more we can hear and learn from Him.

APPLICATION

Are you lacking wisdom in any area of your life? Why not take time to ask God, like Solomon did? He is more than happy to give it to you!

CHAPTER 8

MOVING WITH THE RIGHT PEOPLE

'The company you keep has an influence on how you think and who you become.'

–Marina Abraham.

I knew a guy at university called Jerry. He was the first member of his family to get a degree and now enjoys a great job with a great salary.

It's hard to believe that he left home at the age of 15, having lived a reckless life hanging out with the wrong crowd. Fortunately for him, when his parents could not bear his destructive lifestyle anymore, his dad persuaded Jerry's uncle to take him in. The uncle was a high school teacher in another city with a son of the same age.

Being in a different environment where he had to live with a new family and make new school friends was the turning point for Jerry. He started mixing with a different type of crowd, he had more structure to his home life, including study time and strict routines for bedtime and getting up in the morning.

For once he was mixing with people who had ambitions and dreams, and disciplined themselves in order to attain them. In the past, he had been surrounded by people who lived life like there was nothing really to live for. Jerry says, 'Thank God for the opportunity He gave me. I thank God for where I am today; I might otherwise have been dead by now.' His story made a deep impression on my heart, and inspired this chapter.

YOUR ENVIRONMENT AFFECTS YOU

The environment in which we live and grow up, the people we mix with and listen to, all have a great impact on who we become. I was at a training course recently and the trainer said that environment accounts for 50 percent of what a person will become.

I have the privilege of mixing with different teenagers every week in various projects, and my experience tells me that trainer is right. People really are likely to behave and be like those they hang around with.

If you know that you need to change your thinking, attitude and behaviours, you probably need to think about the people you're spending time with and the environments that influence you.

In his letter to the Corinthians, the apostle Paul advises that 'bad company corrupts good character' (1 Corinthians 15:33). If you know that you need to change your thinking, attitude and behaviours, you probably need to think about the people you're spending time with and the environments that influence you.

As W. Clement Stone puts it, 'You are a product of your environment. So choose the environment that will best develop you toward your objective... Are the things around you helping you toward success or are they holding you back?'

CHOOSE YOUR ENVIRONMENT CAREFULLY

Not everybody can have the opportunity that Jerry had of being put into a new situation for a fresh start. But as you read this book, I encourage you to reflect on who and what in your environment is likely to hinder your growth.

As a teen, you must carefully and deliberately choose your friends and the people you relate to. Who are your friends? How much will your relationship with them influence you or

As a teen, you must carefully and deliberately choose your friends and the people you relate to.

your future? What can you do to improve your relationship with the people around you? Is it worth the effort, or should you move away from these friends? Is the school you go to helping you get to where you ought to be? You can't answer all these questions straight away, but reflect on them from time to time. They will help you to understand some of your problems, aspirations and concerns.

FIND LIKE-MINDED PEOPLE

As a teen, there is a tendency to want to follow the crowd and do what everyone else seems to be doing. Not so for you who wants to get to the palace. Knowledge is power, so, armed with the knowledge that the palace is the best place to be in life, spend your time with good people who think like you, who seem to know why they are here, who have ambition for higher things.

You can find such people amongst your peers at school, your neighbourhood, your cousins, at church, in your sports teams or other hobbies. You may admire their success, or you may see that their family has the kind of values you aspire to have. You won't find them amongst the kids who are disrupting lessons or using drugs. Where can you imagine their lives going?

To get to your palace, you don't necessarily have to keep company with your own age group the whole time. All you need is to identify where you aspire to go or be and identify the people around you who can get you there. These things don't just happen by chance.

One of the benefits of moving with the right people in your journey to the palace is that you can study together or brainstorm on how to solve a problem together. Their wisdom and experience can point the way for you and motivate you.

In an age of technology, distance is no barrier to what useful information you can share with each other. You can meet friends online who share your goals, or join forums to learn more about the experiences of others. But always remember to stay safe online: people are not always who they say they are, so don't arrange to meet or give out any personal information.

I remember my pastor describing how there was a friendly competition between him and his friends as new Christians to grow in the Lord . They would give themselves a target as to how many scriptures they could memorise, or how many chapters of the Bible they could read in a day. This 'team target' motivated each of them to do their best, and they all grew in faith as a result.

THE RISKS OF MOVING WITH THE WRONG CROWD

Many teenagers miss opportunities in life–and some even lose their lives–as a result of the company they keep. In the UK, crime statistics are released

Many teenagers miss opportunities in life - and some even lose their lives - as a result of the company they keep.

annually and they show that in one year alone, over 125,000 young people were arrested. 33,000 of these went to court for sentencing, and over 2,000 were taken into custody. The average length of a custodial sentence for this age group was 14.5 months.

Of course, most teenagers do not end up in prison or with criminal records, but a great many run the risk! And many of their destinies – both boys' and girls'–are cut short by the impact of teenage pregnancy, or the use of drugs and alcohol, all of which can lead to depression and other illnesses.

> *Choose to move with those who truly have the fear of the Lord, and your destiny is secured. Your move to the palace is sure too.*

There are many teens who have made it to their palaces just by moving with and being influenced by the right company early in life. The choice is yours. Remember, your choices can make or break you. Choose to move with those who truly have the fear of the Lord, and your destiny is secured. Your move to the palace is sure too.

Does it mean that if you do bad things you won't make it to the palace? Certainly not. Some people start down the wrong road but later get back on track. (The disadvantage is that they have fewer years to enjoy a palace life.) Maybe some die or battle major illness before they have a chance to turn their lives around. A lot just settle for a mediocre life because they have been led to believe it is the best that life can offer them.

You are certainly not in these categories. Reading this book gives you an edge, to choose where you belong and what you want. Like a salvation decision, no one can make this decision for you.

APPLICATION

Why not take a minute to list people whose company you keep, and examine the effect of these relationships in your life?

CHAPTER 9

DEVELOP THE RIGHT CHARACTER AND ATTITUDE

'Moral character makes for smooth travelling; an
evil life is a hard life.' -Proverbs 11:5

Your character is your real self: who you truly are, who you are when nobody is watching. It is much more than just the impression you give to others. As Abraham Lincoln said, 'Character is like a tree and reputation like its shadow.'

Character is the combination of all the qualities, flaws and traits that make up a person. We tend to notice the people who seem to be 'really good' or 'really bad' characters. In fact, we all have some good characteristics and some bad characteristics. It is normal to have flaws in your character but you can certainly work on them! To get to your palace,

> *Character is the combination of all the qualities, flaws and traits that make up a person.*

you need to make the most of the good parts of your character, and work on leaving behind the not-so-good parts.

The kind of character you have will determine how you respond to both the positive and the negative situations that you will face throughout your life.

THE BENEFITS OF BEING OF GOOD CHARACTER

Good character includes having the right attitude, integrity, loyalty, trustworthiness, truthfulness, humility, a spirit of excellence, dependability, attention to detail, and discipline in all spheres of your life.

Being of good character differentiates you from the crowd, it is the foundation of your success story.

The people around us notice our characters. They are either drawn towards us or avoid us on the strength of our character. They recommend us to others or criticise us on the strength of our character.

HOW A BAD CHARACTER CAN HOLD YOU BACK

A lot of people lack integrity; they lie at any opportunity; spend money carelessly; eat voraciously; steal from others, make promises they do not mean. The list could go on and on.

Even if you have many qualities such as intelligence, good looks and wit, if you lack good character you will not reach your potential. Your flaws will suddenly cause you to stumble.

If you get a top degree and have the best work experience in the world, people will be reluctant to employ you if they have reason to doubt your character. Every employer out there is looking for people of good character and attitude to trust with their business. It's more valuable

> *If you get a top degree and have the best work experience in the world, people will be reluctant to employ you if they have reason to doubt your character.*

than the skills you offer, because skills can be taught with training. But only you can work on your character to make it better.

Bad character can also cause people to withdraw friendship from you. Good parents do not want their children to associate with peers whose character is questionable, who do not seem trustworthy.

CHARACTERISTICS TO STRIVE FOR

Consider how these three characteristics could make a difference to your life:

1   HUMILITY

Humility is the opposite of arrogance, pride and boastfulness. It is a recognition that your gifts and achievements

> *Jesus, our saviour, is our model of good character.*

come from God. Jesus, our saviour, is our model of good character. He was humble even to death. God resists the proud and raises the humble.

To be humble is to accept when you are wrong and to apologise when necessary. It helps you to value and help others, and accept your own shortcomings. Being humble does not deny you of your self-worth; instead, like Jesus, it will bring you to your palace.

2   PERSEVERANCE

Sporting heroes will tell you that continuous practice and determination got them to where they are now. Were there times they did not feel like practising? Certainly! But they pressed on. That attitude got them to their palaces.

As a teen and student, you will get better grades when you are diligent about your study. Sometimes the work seems so difficult, but with perseverance, you will get there.

As long as you do not give up, I cannot see what will stop you from achieving your palace dream as a teen. Thomas Edison, the great American inventor said, 'Our greatest weakness lies in giving up. The most certain way to succeed is always to try just one more time.'

3   COMMITMENT TO EXCELLENCE

The person with an attitude of excellence is the one who gets the prize.

The person with an attitude of excellence is the one who gets the prize. In everything you do from today as you read this book, do it with the mind of leaving a mark of excellence behind. Perhaps up until now, you have approached things in a haphazard way or with little effort. Leave that attitude behind. If you plant an excellent seed now, you will harvest an excellent result later.

If you plant an excellent seed now, you will harvest an excellent result later.

Put a mark of excellence in all your school work as a teen. In your line of calling, work towards the excellence that can bring you to the top. Many aspire to be at the top, but they refuse to do what it takes.

As Vince Lombardi, the former American football player and coach put it, 'the quality of a person's life is in direct proportion to their commitment to excellence, regardless of their chosen field of endeavour.'

A spirit of excellence does not mean that you have to be able to achieve everything brilliantly, but that you approach everything with the best of your efforts.

ROLE MODELS

1   Read the Bible to emulate the character of successful people, above all that of Jesus, who is our first mentor.

Joseph became the prime minister of Egypt because he understood that as a teen he was heading for the palace, and therefore there were certain things he could not do. He decided to stay on course and live by Godly principles. He was tempted to sleep with Potiphar's wife, but he chose to uphold his good character as he wanted to make the best of his life (Genesis 39-41). So can you! As a teen, do not yield to a temptation that could smear your good name, even if you think no-one will find out.

2   Look to the people whose character you admire. Model yourself on them.
3   Read books by successful people to determine their key characteristics.
4   Pray that you will overcome your weaknesses and become a better person every day.

HOW YOUR ATTITUDE INFLUENCES YOUR CHARACTER

The great physicist Albert Einstein said, 'Weakness of attitude becomes weakness of character.' Developing the right attitude is crucial. As we looked at in chapter two, your mind and thoughts play a huge part in determining your success.

It takes faith to believe that you can be what you dream of. Many will say that faith is a difficult thing to have when you face challenges in life. That's true, but the Lord requires us to have unwavering faith, which only He gives. He needs people to rely absolutely on His promises, and with that attitude to obtain their reward.

CHARACTER CAN BE DEVELOPED

Benjamin Franklin, one of the Founding Fathers of the United States, designed a plan to build his own character. He identified thirteen qualities he wanted to improve on and devised how he would achieve it. He focused on one per month, constantly practised and within a year, he had achieved his goal in all thirteen areas! Why not try it too? Focus, determination and diligence is the key.

Bradley Whitford said, 'Infuse your life with action. Don't wait for it to happen. Make it happen. Make your own future.'

APPLICATION

Why not take a moment to list the characteristics you want to uphold or discard, and draw up a plan as to how you will achieve this?

CHAPTER 10

OBEY GOD

———————— ⚜ ————————

'If you are willing and obedient, you shall eat the good of the land,'- Isaiah 1:19.

One of my favourite phrases from the Bible is 'obedience is better than sacrifice' (1 Samuel 15:22). It is better to obey God than to be disobedient and try to appease Him by offering other sacrifices, as King Saul did. God made it clear in 1 Samuel 2:30 that He honours those who honour Him, and He has contempt for those who dishonour Him.

Walking with God in obedience is like a child who obeys his or her parents in all things. Good parents will always be willing to provide the best for such a child. When a person

When a person walks in obedience to God, there is a certain assurance that they too will have a 'happy ending'.

walks in obedience to God, there is a certain assurance that they too will have a 'happy ending'. To move from teen to palace, you will need to cooperate with God your creator because the Scriptures tell us that without Him, we can do nothing (John 15:5).

KNOW GOD

We have already established that the first step toward a palace dream is to give your life to Jesus Christ, that is, accept Jesus into your life and build a father/child relationship with him. That does not mean that you won't make mistakes sometimes, but where you have a relationship with God, you can always say, 'Lord, I am sorry,' and He will forgive you and continue to shower you with His unfailing love.

When you do not have Jesus in your life, even if you get to your palace, you may not be able to sustain yourself. Without His help, you may fall. If not, you may only succeed in attaining earthly rewards and missing out on eternal blessings.

There are so many tragic stories of rich and successful people who take their own lives, go bankrupt, have broken relationships and the like. A lot of these people did not know God; they had not established a relationship with God that would sustain them. Some may have heard about Jesus Christ, His love and saving power, but the message fell on deaf ears.

WHAT GOD WANTS

A lot of people claim to believe in God, but it is not enough just to believe in God. We must also obey Him. God desires our obedience, our total obedience. King Saul lost his kingship as a result of partial obedience (1 Samuel 15:25).

Because God desires full obedience from us, in Isaiah 1:19 He gives us the promise that anyone who is obedient will 'eat the good of our land', that is, be well provided for. In your case it means that as a teen, your obedience to God will get you to your palace.

You may wonder what it means to obey God. We read in Deuteronomy 28:1 that it is to obey His commandments and observe them diligently.

The next question you may want to ask is 'how can we know His commandments?' In Joshua 1:8, God explains that by meditating on His word all the time, Joshua will learn to do what is right, which will bring him success.

The secret to knowing God's commandments is to study the Word of God, so it becomes food for your soul. For those of you who may not know, the Word of God is found in the Bible. Reading, studying and meditating on it is a major step towards showing obedience to God, because the same commandment He gave to Joshua, He is giving to us all.

Another way of showing that you obey God is by following in the footsteps of His son, our role model, Jesus Christ. God sent Him to this world to become man. He died so that our sins could be forgiven, and He also showed us how to live.

PRAYER IS THE KEY

One of the ways Jesus taught us to establish a relationship with (and be obedient to) God was through prayer. Prayer is the essential foundation of every Christian's life. It is the way we communicate with God. Our heart speaks to His heart, we feel His presence, we sense His guidance, we come to know more of Him and of ourselves.

Prayer does not only keep you in tune with God: it brings you God's blessings, and it helps to keep the devil at bay. It was Jesus' prayer for Peter that kept Satan from sifting Peter away (Luke 22:31). Because of Jesus' prayer life, the devil could not interfere with His destiny no matter how much he tried.

Prayer does not only keep you in tune with God: it brings you God's blessings, and it helps to keep the devil at bay.

Jesus began and ended His earthly ministry with prayer. It was this example that prompted His disciples to ask Him how to pray (Luke 11:1). The Bible emphasises the need for prayer both as obedience and as a source of blessing in a lot of chapters.

For a teenager aspiring to the palace, you must make time to communicate with God, so as to receive guidance for your next step.

PREVALENT SINS AMONGST TEENS

Whenever someone disobeys God, that person has sinned. God loves His children, but He despises their sins. Sin can make God turn His back on His children. Many sins are mentioned in the

Bible, but we are going to look at a couple that are particularly prevalent among teens: sexual impurity and drug / alcohol abuse.

SEX IS A PRECIOUS GIFT

If you are determined to live in a palace, you must stay away from premarital sexual relationships. (A premarital sexual relationship means to have sex before you are married.) Nor is it acceptable to be physically intimate with someone and stop just short of having sex.

God created sex as a great blessing. It offers married couples an intimate, joyful union, and enables them to share in His creative power when used to bring new life into the world. Because it is such an awesome gift, it must be used according to God's design for us. When we misuse powerful things, there can be terrible consequences.

To engage in premarital sex is to sin against the creator of your body. The Bible says in 1 Corinthians 6:19 that our bodies are the place where the Holy Spirit lives. So to engage in premarital sex is to defile the temple (home) of the Holy Spirit.

Tempting you to engage in premature sexual relationships is a key weapon the devil uses to hinder your destiny, and that is why we see it so often among teenagers. Flee from it, for it causes the Holy Spirit (who is your helper, inspirer, guide, strength, and guard) to be dormant. The apostle Paul explains that the Spirit can be grieved (Ephesians 4:30).

When the Holy Spirit is chased away by this act, your body is not simply left vacant. An evil spirit can come and occupy its place.

The evil spirit will lie to you, it wants to mislead and destroy you. I know countless teenagers whose destinies were thwarted by this sin. Many had to go through a series of deliverance meetings to be restored, but in every case there were consequences.

CONSEQUENCES OF PRE-MARITAL SEX

Some of the obvious consequences of a premarital sexual relationship are: having children out of wedlock; having children by different fathers; being a single parent; raising children with challenging behaviours because they lack a strong father figure; the difficulties in being a very young, inexperienced mother; an increase in crime rates in the community as a result of unstable families; the epidemic of sexually transmitted diseases which cause terrible physical harm (some of which lead to infertility and even death) and abortion. Abstinence from sex is healthier and safer.

But what about contraception, you may ask? Any health professional or adult will tell you that preventative measures are prone to fail. My mother used the birth control coil to prevent pregnancy, but I was born as the fourth of five children, with a coil in my hand. She could not stop me from coming into the world because she was not God! Neither are you, so be careful. The pain is immeasurable and not worth it. Avoiding any opportunity to sin in this way is the best way.

It's not worth losing your salvation for a five-minute pleasure.

All of these consequences listed above have a lasting effect on both parent and child. We can always seek God's forgiveness and receive His mercy, but the practical effects of our sins in this life cannot always be undone.

A greater consequence still is the eternal effect of our sins. If during an abortion a teenager dies, the chances are that they might go to hell. It's not worth losing your salvation for a five-minute pleasure.

HELP TO STAY PURE

The sexual urge is a strong and natural instinct. But it is possible to stay pure until you are married. Think of practical ways to help you steer clear of temptation: for example, if you start dating someone, talk to them from the start about your values (if you are too embarrassed to discuss these things, then perhaps they are not the right person for you), don't go to a bedroom alone with your boyfriend or girlfriend, don't watch pornography, choose your friends wisely, speak to someone you respect when you are not sure of what to do. Look again at chapter 3 and remember how you can intentionally grow in your life simply by making small changes to your habits and values.

ABUSE OF DRUGS AND ALCOHOL

Another trap for teenagers is the use and abuse of drugs and alcohol. Again, these are a sin against God and bring consequences.

We are told in the sixth commandment that God gave Moses, 'Thou shall not kill' (Exodus 20:13). When you engage in taking drugs, smoking or using alcohol, you are damaging your body, to the point of death. Avoiding these dangers can speed you on your way to the palace. The lives of so many people, including teenagers, have been cut short by these habits.

REJECT ALL SIN

There are many sins, like lying, stealing, jealousy, malice and lack of forgiveness (Galatians 5:19-21). Many seem attractive in the short term, but none of them is good or healthy in the end. It is for every teenager to identify which sins particularly threaten them and to avoid the opportunities to engage in them.

When you choose to obey God, you are telling Him that you love Him with all your heart, that you trust Him, that you believe in Him, and that you are ready to rely on Him. This obedience and trust will bring great blessings to you.

Partial obedience is not the answer. You cannot afford to stay away from some sins and enjoy the pleasure of others. Sin is sin, and no matter how small or big, it hurts either you or others. Partial obedience *Sin is sin.* deprived King Saul of enjoying the benefits of being a king until the end of his life. The Lord called his partial obedience disobedience!

Abraham is an example of a man who fully obeyed God. As a result, in Genesis 12:2-3, God made a covenant with Abraham to bless him, make him the father of all nations and multiply his descendants. By trusting God, Abraham obeyed Him, and the Lord fulfilled His promises. Today, Christians all over the world are still enjoying the benefit of Abraham's obedience to God. Like Abraham, you can also live an obedient life that will shower blessings on future generations of your family.

THE CHOICE IS YOURS TODAY

> *Your ability to get to your palace from being a teen is in your hands.*

Your ability to get to your palace from being a teen is in your hands. You can choose to know God better and obey Him all the days that you may live, enjoying His promises, or live in sin and disobedience and suffer the consequences.

We can read in Genesis 5:21-24 the story of a man named Enoch, who lived for 365 years, always walking close to God. The Bible records that he did not die, but that God took him straight to heaven (Hebrews 11:5). Enoch's experience is another example of the rewards of obedience that come naturally when we walk God's way.

Teens, the palace awaits you. You CAN become successful, and you will get to your palace. All you need to do is to abide by the principles in this book, and you will be happy you did. If you are yet to give your life to Jesus, you can say this short prayer and start your new life with Jesus today.

Lord Jesus, I repent of my sin, I am sorry for all my shortcomings. I ask you to please come into my life today and take your place in me. Please, help me never to sin again that I may get to my palace on this earth and enjoy eternal life with you in Jesus' name.

APPLICATION

Why not take the next few minutes to identify areas in your life where you have been disobedient to God? Make plans to amend your ways today.

NOTES

Myles Munroe, Understanding Your Potential: Discovering the Hidden You (Destiny image publishers, Inc 2005)

John C. Maxwell, The 15 Invaluable Laws of Growth (Hachette Book Group September, 2014)

Brian Tracy, Eat That Frog (Berrett-Koehler Publishers, 2001).

Mensa Otabil, Buy the Future (Altar International Ltd, 2002).

Joel Osteen, Becoming a Better You: 7 Keys to Improving Your Life Every Day (Simons & Schuster UK Ltd, 2007)

The Complete James Allen Treasury, Mind Is The Master: As a Man Thinketh (Penguin Group Ltd, 2010), 141- 163

The Coaching Academy Training Materials (2013).

ONLINE QUOTES

"Good Read Quotes." Last modified September 30, 2016. http://www.goodreads.com/quotes

"Brainy Quotes." Last modified October 5, 2016 http://www.brainy-quote.com/quotes/quotes

"Inspiration Quotes." Last Modified October 10, 2016, http://www.values.com/inspirational-quotes

"Wiki Quotes." Last Modified September 11, 2016, https://en.wikiquote.org.

"Wikipedia." Last Modified September 11, 2016, https://en.wikipedia.org/wiki/Choice

"Goggle Search." Last Modified October 11, 2016, https://www.google.co.uk/search

ARTICLES

Amy Willis, "This incredible 21-year-old can play musical instruments with his eyes," Metro Newspaper, October 21, 2015, accessed October 21, 2015, http://metro.co.uk/2015/10/21

Harry Readhead, "Kids Who Spend More Than 3 Hours a Day on Social Media More Likely to Have Mental Health," Metro

Newspaper, 20, October 2015, accessed 20, October 2015, http://
metro.co.uk/2015/10/20

Father Raniero Cantalamessa, "The Fear of The Lord," June 21,
2008, http://www.catholic.org/news/international/europe/story.
php?id=28326

Ministry of Justice and Youth Justice Board for England and Wales,

"The National Statistics Youth justice annual statistics: 2013 to
2014" First published: January 29, 2015,

file:///C:/Users/JDC%2001/AppData/Local/Microsoft/
Windows/INetCache/IE/TDMK65MN/youth-justice-stats-exec-
summary-2.pdf

ONLINE DICTIONARIES

The online Oxford dictionary, Last accessed, October 16, 2015
https://en.oxforddictionaries.com/

The Online Merriam- Webster Dictionary, Last accessed September
11, 2016, http: www.merriam-webster.com/

BIBLE REFERENCES

INTRODUCTION

1 Peter 1:9

1. THE SEED OF GREATNESS

Genesis 1:26

Genesis 1:24

Ephesians 2:10

Proverbs 18:16

Genesis 40

Jeremiah 1:5

John 3:3

2. IT STARTS FROM THE MIND

Romans 12:2

Proverbs 23:7

Genesis 1:31

Romans 10:17

Proverbs 4:23

Proverbs 4:23

Hebrews 11:1.

Matthew 19: 26

Genesis 39:19-21

Genesis 37:9

3. PLAN FOR INTENTIONAL GROWTH

Psalm 139:14
Ecclesiastes 3:1-8
John 15:5

4. SET GOALS IN YOUR LIFE

Habakkuk 2:2-3

5. MAKE THE RIGHT CHOICES

Genesis 25:29-34
Joshua 24:14-15

6. SEEK KNOWLEDGE

Hosea 4:6
Daniel 1:17

7. GROWING IN WISDOM

Proverbs 8:11
Proverbs 13:10
I Corinthians 3:19
James 3:17
Proverbs 1:17

James 1:5

1 Kings 5:12

8. MOVING WITH THE RIGHT PEOPLE

1 Corinthians 15:33

9. DEVELOP THE RIGHT CHARACTER
AND ATTITUDE

Proverbs 11:5

Genesis 39-41

10. OBEY GOD

Isaiah 1:19

1 Samuel 15:22

1 Samuel 2:30

John 15:5 (Paraphrased because 'me' is changed to 'Him')

Deuteronomy 28:1

Joshua 1:8

Luke 22:31

Luke 11:1

1 Corinthians 6:19

Ephesians 4:30

Exodus 20:13

Galatians 5:19-21

Genesis 12:2-3

Genesis 5:21-24
Hebrews 11:5

Lightning Source UK Ltd.
Milton Keynes UK
UKOW06f0816100917

308861UK00006B/127/P